YOUR KNOWLEDGE HAS VALUE

Lasse Skaksen

Transformational vs Transactional in creating LMX relationships

GRIN Verlag

Bibliografische Information der Deutschen Nationalbibliothek:

Die Deutsche Bibliothek verzeichnet diese Publikation in der Deutschen National-
bibliografie; detaillierte bibliografische Daten sind im Internet über http://dnb.d-
nb.de/ abrufbar.

Imprint:

Copyright © 2011 GRIN Verlag GmbH
Druck und Bindung: Books on Demand GmbH, Norderstedt Germany
ISBN: 978-3-656-49534-5

This book at GRIN:

http://www.grin.com/en/e-book/232611/transformational-vs-transactional-in-crea-
ting-lmx-relationships

GRIN - Your knowledge has value

Der GRIN Verlag publiziert seit 1998 wissenschaftliche Arbeiten von Studenten, Hochschullehrern und anderen Akademikern als eBook und gedrucktes Buch. Die Verlagswebsite www.grin.com ist die ideale Plattform zur Veröffentlichung von Hausarbeiten, Abschlussarbeiten, wissenschaftlichen Aufsätzen, Dissertationen und Fachbüchern.

Visit us on the internet:

http://www.grin.com/

http://www.facebook.com/grincom

http://www.twitter.com/grin_com

From:	Lasse T. Skaksen	Course:	Leadership
Subject:	Argumentative Essay	Date:	17/04 - 2011

Table of Contents

Some researchers argue that transformational leadership is more effective than transactional leadership in developing high-quality leader-follower (LMX) relationships in order to influence followers' job performance and job satisfaction. Do you agree or disagree with this statement? Justify your position and arguments

1. Position:

Based on a thorough literature search I take the position that transformational leadership is not necessarily more effective in developing high-quality leader-follower (LMX) relationships than transactional leadership. I argue that there is no such thing as a universal applicable leadership style and that, among others, cultural situational factors determines the most effective leadership style.

2. Introduction

Business today is more competitive and global than ever. Hence greater challenges are imposed on businesses and their leaders at all levels. Companies are forced to be more efficient and effective, i.e. maximize outcome from available resources. Within leadership theory it has repeatedly been established that high-quality LMX relationships increases employee's performance, i.e. maximizes output. (Wang et al., 2005)(Lussier & Achua, 2010). I.e. developing high-quality LMX relationships, are a means to optimize business performance. In this essay I will utilize motivational theories to support my argument that the quality of LMX relationship, affects followers job performance and satisfaction.

As mentioned companies are furthermore facing global challenges, thus also the challenge of leading employees from different cultures and different countries. In recognized literature it is established that: different cultures should be managed in different ways (Gerstner & Days, 1994) and in order to succeed leadership style should be adapted to the cultural situation (Dorfman & Howell, 1997). Thus if companies want to optimize the quality of LMX relationships, they must adopt the leadership style according to the culture.

In this essay I will utilize three of Hofstede's renowned cultural dimensions[1] (Hofstede, 1993) to argue that transformational leadership is not always superior in establishing high-quality LMX relationships. In this essay, when referring to transactional and transformational leadership, I will be referring to the definition given by the "Rosetta stone" of leadership theory, Bernhard Bass (Bass, 1985).

3. LMX relationships influence on followers job satisfaction and job performance

It is commonly accepted and well documented in peer reviewed literature that there is a positive relationship between high-quality LMX relationship, followers' job performance and satisfaction. Lussier and Achua argue that high-quality LMX relationships, leads to not only higher job satisfaction and performance but also lower follower turnover (Lussier and Achua. 2010 Based on Gagnon and Michael 2004, Mueller and Lee 2002, Erdogan and Kraimer 2004).

High-quality LMX relationships are furthermore characterized by increased levels of leader support, guidance, mutual trust and obligations – this is exactly what high-quality LMX relationships are build on. (Lussier and Achua 2010. Graen & Uhl-Bien 1995). LMX relationships are a dyadic process, and hence build on behavior/exchanges between two parties. Turning to motivational theories we can conclude that given the above description of the leader characteristics hold, we can infer that at least two of the major motivational theories, *expectancy*

---

[1] Individualism/collectivism, Power Distance, Time orientation, Uncertainty avoidance and Masculinity/Feminity

theory(e.g. Vroom, Porter & Lawler) and *equity theory* (e.g. Adams) can be utilized to argue that high-quality LMX relationships will increase follower satisfaction and performance.

Within expectancy theory it is a key assumption that followers act according to conscious expectations that a particular behavior will lead to specific desirable goals. (Vroom. 1964) With the definition of high-quality LMX in mind, we can argue that in high-quality LMX relationships, leaders are better able to identify what exactly is a desirable goal for the follower and set goals accordingly.

Equity Theory is based on the main assumption that followers level of motivation is mainly defined by the perception of own rewards AND the rewards other receive, i.e. not the reward itself but more so the comparison with the rewards received by others.(Adams, 1965) With increased leader support, mutual trust and obligations in high-quality LMX relationships, we can argue that the follower will be treated at least fairly and maybe even better than others, thus increasing motivation and thereby job performance and satisfaction. Equal treatment is a cornerstone of transactional leadership, i.e. transactional leadership is suitable to develop high-quality LMX. (Mumin Dayan, 2009, Pillai et al. 1999) I.e. the creation of in and out groups is minimized (if at all there) under transactional leadership, as opposed to transactional. See more under 5.0 in the essay.

4. Transactional leadership and building high-quality LMX relationships; culture as situational factor. [2]

Given that businesses are operating in an increasingly globalised world, one must accept that culture is almost always a significant situational factor, thus I argue that the three following factors are key determinants of the appropriate leadership style.

4.1 Power Distance and transactional leadership

In cultures with high power distance, the follower expects the leader to lead. Followers with high power distance will be confused or frustrated if the leader fails to lead, and the quality of LMX relationship will suffer accordingly. Thus transactional leadership is more appropriate as the transactional leader clearly specifies the followers' task, what is expected from the follower and what rewards/punishments the followers' behavior/performance will lead to. Examples of

---

[2] I assume that Hofstede's cultural dimensions are well known; hence I will not elaborate or define these.

countries with high power distance are China, including Hong Kong SAR, Japan and most other Asian countries. Leaders that due to their autocratic and task focused behavior in low power distance countries will be perceived negatively by followers, will in high power distance countries be perceived as capable, successful and as good leaders.(Brazier, 2005. Dorfman & Howell, 1995)

4.2 Uncertainty Avoidance

Transactional leaders define tasks, goals, performance and behavior expectations very clearly, i.e. uncertainty is minimized for the follower. Followers with high uncertainty avoidance feel uncomfortable in unstructured situations and appreciate the well defined guidelines given by the leader. (www.geert-hofstede.com). By minimizing experienced uncertainty for the follower, the leader builds trust and respect. At the same time the follower is better able to perform, i.e. builds trust and respect with the leader, which among others defines a high-quality LMX relationship. With expectancy theory and the findings by House (House, 1995) in mind, it is even clearer that a leader's failure to clearly identify and structure what is expected and how rewards are distributed will de-motivate followers. Transactional leadership is by definition superior to transformational in clearly defining tasks and rewards systems.

4.3 Individualism/Collectivism

Transactional leadership can be argued to be more effective in both individualistic as well as collectivistic cultures. In collectivistic cultures it is expected that a leader considers what is best for "we" instead of "I". I.e. a transactional leader that does not seek to lead by charisma is perceived more positive by followers. The charismatic leader risks being perceived as trying to promote own interests before the groups. (Dorfman & Howell, 1997). A charismatic leader will not receive support from followers in a collectivistic culture as they do not wish to "stand out" and dislikes the leaders need to "stand out" from the group. The leader will be disappointed by the lack of commitment and motivation from followers and followers will feel the leader is "endangering" them by attempting to single them out from the group – which leads to lower mutual trust and respect, i.e. lower quality LMX relationship.

In individualistic cultures followers are motivated by achieving own goals and value these higher than common goals for the group (www.geert-hofstede.com). When a transactional leader defines a fair and challenging reward systems, that challenges the individualistic follower, the follower will perceive the leader as taking his/her needs into consideration. This is very much in line with expectancy theory (e.g. Vroom, Porter & Lawler) and the argument that individuals are motivated by clearly defined desirable and realistic goals. (Vroom, 1964)

The above arguments all emanate from the consideration that in contemporary global business, culture should be considered as a situational factor. I would like to place a cautions remark to the theories and concepts above. All of the above theories and concepts are based on western leadership theories and surveys, which not necessarily holds in non western countries. (Brain and Lewis, 2004. Blunt and Jones, 1997) In order for the arguments to be completely valid, further research in non western countries has to be conducted. It has recently been established in a study that participative leadership, i.e. non transactional, can actually motivate in China (Tse et al., 2005), which actually opposes my findings above – e.g. with regards to uncertainty avoidance. This finding is interesting and should be examined further, especially considering the coming new world order, with China and India as superpowers.

5.0 Equal treatment

In addition to the argument that culture is a significant situational factor in deciding appropriate leadership, I will argue that a key component of transactional leadership is the innate feature that followers are treated equally. (Bass, 1985) This minimizes the risk of in and out-groups, where the overall LMX quality suffers, which goes for all cultures (Piccolo et al.). Furthermore I will argue that in collectivistic and high uncertainty avoidance cultures, this innate features has an overall positive effect on LMX quality, even though the individual LMX relationship may suffer.

6.0 Conclusion

From the above presented arguments I conclude that transactional leadership in some scenarios is more effective in building high-quality LMX relationships. The arguments above are based on the fact that culture is a significant situational factor in contemporary global business environment. It is concluded that in, all others equal, high power distance, high uncertainty avoidance and both individualistic and collectivistic cultures/countries transactional leadership is superior to transformational leadership. The innate feature that transactional leaders treat followers equally is a key argument. The perception of fairness is valued in all cultures, and even though the quality of a LMX relationship to one follower may decrease, the overall LMX quality level will increase. Lastly, the two main arguments were combined in underlining that the "equality" principle in transactional leadership, is especially desirable in collectivistic and high uncertainty avoidance cultures.

Lastly I will state the above should not be interpreted as an argument that transactional leadership is the ONE best leadership approach. Combinations of leadership styles are preferable in all situations.

7.0 References

- Adams, J. S. (1965) Inequity in social exchange. Advances in experimental social Psychology Quarterly, 2, 267 - 299.

- Bass, B. M. (1985). Leadership and performance beyond expectations. New York: Free Press.

- Blunt, P. and Jones, M. L. (1997) Exploring the limits of western leadership theory in Ease Asia and Africa, Personnel Review, 26, pp. 6.

- Brain, K. and Lewis, D. (2004) Exploring leadership preferences in multicultural workgroups: an Australian case study, The Leadership & Organisation Development Journal, 25, 3, pp. 263-278.

- Brazier, D. K. (2005) Influence of contextual factors on health-care leadership, Leadership and Organisation Development Journal, 26, 2, pp. 128-140.

- Dorfman, W & Howell, P 1997, 'Leadership in Western and Asian countries: commonalities and differences in effective leadership processes across cultures', Leadership Quarterly, vol. 8, no. 3, pp. 233-274.

- Gernster, C & Day, D 1994, 'Cross-cultural comparison of leadership prototypes', Leadership Quarterly, vol. 5, no. 2, pp. 121-134.

- Graen, G, Uhl-Bien, M, 1995. 'Relationship-based approach to leadership: development of leader-member exchange (LMX) theory of leadership over 25 years: applying a multi-level multi-domain perspective', Leadership Quarterly, vol. 6, no. 2, pp. 219-247.

- House, R 1971, 'A Path Goal Theory of Leader Effectiveness', Administrative Science Quarterly, Vol. 16, No. 3, pp. 321-339.

- Hofstede, Geert: "Cultural constraints in management theories", 1993, Academy of Management Executive, vol. 7, no. 1, pp. 81-94.

- Lussier, Robert & Achua, Christopher. 2010, Leadership. Theory Application & Skill Development 4e. South Western – Cengage Learning

- Mumin Dayan, C. A. D. B. M. C. (2009) Managerial trust in new product development projects: its antecedents and consequences. R&D Management, 39, 1,pp. 21-37.

- Piccolo, R., Bardes, M., Mayer, D. & Judge, T. (2008) Does high quality leader-member exchange accentuate the effects of organizational justice? European Journal of Work & Organizational Psychology, 17, 2,pp. 26.

- PILIAI, R., SCHRIESHEIM, C. A. & WILLIAMS, E. S. (1999) Fairness Perceptions and Trust as Mediators for Transformational and Transactional Leadership: A Two-Sample Study. Journal of Management, 25, 6,pp. 897.

- Tse, H. M., Dasborough, M. T., & Ashkanasy, N. M. (2005). The role of affect, fairness and social perception in team member exchange. In N. M. Ashkanasy, C. E. J Härtel, & W. J. Zerbe (Eds.), Research on emotion in organisations: The effect of affect in organisational settings (Vol 1, pp.143-171). Oxford, UK: Elsevier

- Victor H. Vroom. "Work and motivation" "New York : John Wiley, cop. 1964

- Wang, H., Law, K. S., Hackett, R. D., Wang, D. and Chen, Z. X. (2005) Leader-member exchange as a mediator of the relationship between transformational leadership and followers' performance and organisational citizenship behaviour, Academy of Management Journal, 48, 3, pp. 420-432.

- www.geert-hofstede.com Gert Hofstede own website.